SOUND INNOVATIONS

for CONCERT BAND

A Revolutionary Method for Intermediate Musicians

Robert **SHELDON** | Peter **BOONSHAFT** | Dave **BLACK** | Bob **PHILLIPS**

Congratulations! You have successfully completed Book 1 and are ready to begin Book 2 of *Sound Innovations*. As you progress through this book, you will develop many new skills. You will continue to learn terms, playing techniques, key signatures, time signatures, and how to improve your reading skills while performing more challenging music. You'll also become more skilled at evaluating and appreciating the music you listen to and create.

Participation in your school's music program will provide you with wonderful experiences. You may want to play classical music, jazz, rock, or pop. You will have fantastic opportunities to play in concert bands, orchestras, jazz bands, and chamber music ensembles. Many students will choose to take private instruction on their instrument.

You may pursue a career in music, or just make music an important part of your life by attending concerts, playing in a community band, or supporting the arts. Wherever music takes you, playing your instrument for a lifetime is a great experience we hope you enjoy.

Sincerely,

Robert Sheldon, Peter Boonshaft, Dave Black, and Bob Phillips

Practice *Sound Innovations* with SmartMusic® Interactive Software

Transform the way you practice. Instead of practicing alone, you play with background accompaniment and hear how your part fits within the whole. *And*, you get instant feedback. You see which notes you've played right or wrong and hear a recording of your performance. Download SmartMusic at **www.smartmusic.com** to get started.

The MP3 CD includes recorded accompaniments for every line of music in your *Sound Innovations* book. Featuring members of your instrument family, these recordings can be played with the included SI Player, easily uploaded to your MP3 player or transferred to your computer. Additionally, many CD and DVD players are equipped to play MP3s directly from the disc. To play an accompaniment, simply choose the file that corresponds to the line of music in the book. Each line has been numbered and named for easy reference.

Also included on the MP3 CD is the SI Player *with* Tempo Change Technology. The SI Player features the ability to change the speed of the recordings without changing pitch—slow the tempo down for practice or speed it up to performance tempo! Use this program to easily play the included MP3 files or any audio file on your computer.

Instrument photos courtesy of Yamaha Corporation of America Band & Orchestral Division
CD Recorded and Mixed at The Lodge Recording Studios, Indianapolis, IN
Performance on CD by: Allen Miller–Trumpet; Carl Lenthe–Trombone and Euphonium;
    Kent Leslie–French Horn; Paul Carlson–Tuba
Accompaniments Written and Recorded by: Kenneth Lampl and Mitchell McCarthy
Ensembles and *Sound Innovations Fanfare for Band* Performed by:
    American Symphonic Winds, Anthony Maiello, Conductor
Production Company: Specialized Personnel Locators
Engineer: Kendall S. Thomsen
DVD Filming and Production: Alfred Music Publishing's New Media Department
Filmed and Recorded at:
    Sound City Center, Van Nuys, CA and The Lodge Recording Studios, Indianapolis, IN

ISBN-10: 0-7390-6758-3
ISBN-13: 978-0-7390-6758-1

Level 1: Sound Review

DVD Please view the DVD for helpful information about practice and performance skills, refer to the glossary for any terms you may not remember from Book 1, and listen to track 1 on the CD for your tuning note.

2 **A NEW BEGINNING**—*Play these notes you already know. Refer to the fingering chart if you need help. Name the key. Point to the following:*

- *bass clef*
- *a measure*
- *repeat sign*
- *a bar line*
- *a whole note*
- *fermata*
- *a breath mark*
- *time signature*
- *final bar line*
- *a half note*

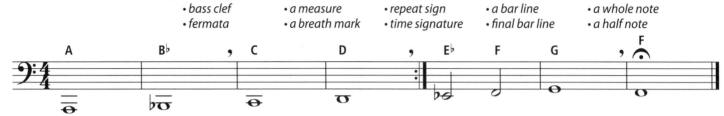

3 **FAMILIAR PLACES**—*Place the corresponding letter in the space nearest the appropriate note or symbol:*

- A. whole note
- B. half note
- C. quarter note
- D. tie
- E. whole rest
- F. half rest
- G. quarter rest
- H. tempo marking

4 **LIGHTLY ROW**—*What is the time signature? How many beats are in each measure? What kind of note gets one beat (count)? Name the key.*

Traditional

5 **STARLIGHT DUET**—*What is a duet? Can you name the piece on which this duet is based? Choose to play either the top line or the bottom line, then switch parts on the repeat.* **DVD**

Adapted by W. A. Mozart (1756–1791)

6 **LONDON BRIDGE**—*Clap the rhythm as you count the beats, then sing the piece before you play. As in book 1, you can determine appropriate places to breathe. Discuss this with your teacher.*

English Folk Song

7 **A MINOR ADJUSTMENT**—*Play these notes you already know. Refer to the fingering chart if you need help. Notice the key signature. Point to the following:*

- *loud dynamic marking*
- *dotted half note*
- *pickup note*
- *a slur*
- *soft dynamic marking*
- *an eighth note*
- *time signature*
- *an accent*

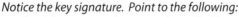

8 **WALTZ OF THE WOODCHUCKS**—*Place the corresponding letter in the space nearest the appropriate note or symbol:*

A. ritardando   B. time signature   C. key signature   D. divisi
E. first ending   F. second ending   G. eighth rest   H. a dotted quarter note

9 **BINGO**—*What is the time signature? How many beats are in each measure? What kind of note gets one beat (count)?*

American Folk Song

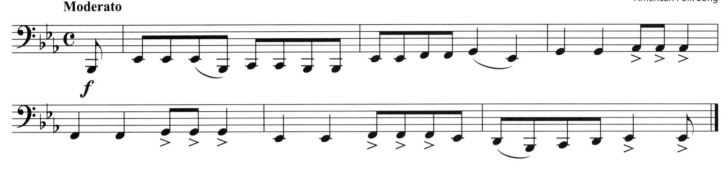

Austrian composer **Johann Strauss, Jr.** (1825–1899), known as "The Waltz King," was largely responsible for the popularity of the waltz in Vienna during the 19th century. Some of his most famous works are *Pizzicato Polka*, *The Blue Danube*, and *Tales from the Vienna Woods*.

10 **SOUTHERN ROSES**—*Name the key. How many beats are in each measure?*

Johann Strauss, Jr. (1825–1899)

11 **MARCH OF THE DUST BUNNIES**—*What does the style marking tell you? How will you play in order to express this mood?*

12 **DYNAMIC PANIC!**—*Play these notes you already know. Refer to the fingering chart if you need help. Name the key. Point to the following:*

• medium-loud dynamic marking   • a staccato marking   • crescendo   • syncopation
• medium-soft dynamic marking   • a legato marking   • decrescendo

13 **MUSIC MANIA**—*Point to the following before playing:*
· *double bar line* · *crescendo* · *multiple-measure rest* · *syncopation* · *diminuendo* · *D.C. (Da Capo) al Fine*

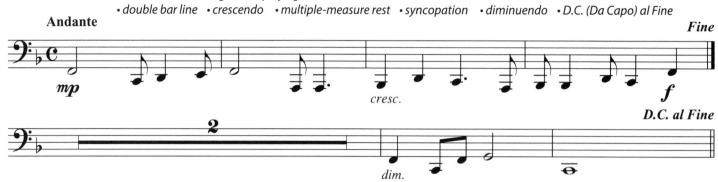

14 **ITSY BITSY SPIDER**—*Play this as a round by having players or groups start every four measures.*

American Traditional

15 **AMERICA (Duet)**—*Switch parts on the repeat.*

American Anthem

16 **CATALPA**—*Name the key and notes before you play. Play this in four-measure phrases.*

Australian Folk Song

17 SMOOTH SAILING—*Play these notes you already know. Refer to the fingering chart if you need help. How long are the phrases?*

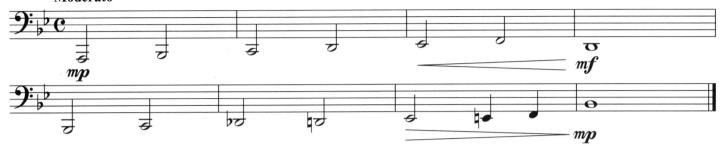

18 A SIGN OF THE TIMES—*Before you play, find the courtesy accidental and the sign for the* D.S. *(Dal Segno) al Fine.*

> **William Billings** (1746–1800), known as the father of American choral music, was one of the first American-born composers. Though he never formally studied music, Billings is credited with developing a uniquely American style of composition.

19 CHESTER—*This American Revolutionary War tune was one of the most popular songs of its time. Name the key before you play. Play this in four-meaure phrases.*

William Billings (1746–1800)

20 BILLY BOY IN SYNC—*Circle the measures with syncopated rhythms. Sing and clap the piece before you play.*

American Folk Song

21 CHROMATIC SCALE—*Review your half-stepping skills. Write the enharmonic note name in the spaces provided below each note.*

22 **F MAJOR SCALE AND ARPEGGIO**—*Practice at a steady tempo at various speeds to increase technical proficiency.* **DVD**

23 **F MAJOR SCALE INTERVAL STUDY**—*Practice at a steady tempo at various speeds to increase technical proficiency.*

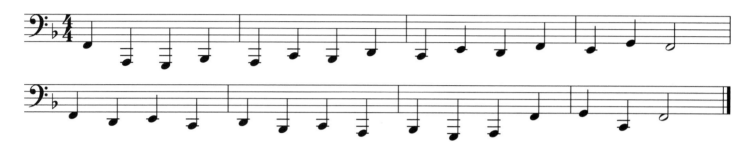

24 **CHORD BUILDER WARM-UP IN F MAJOR**—*Full band arrangement. Listen carefully to how the tone of your instrument blends with the sound of the ensemble.* **DVD**

25 **TONAL WARM-UP IN F MAJOR**—*Listen carefully in order to play in tune and with a good tone.*

26 **TECHNICAL WARM-UP IN F MAJOR**—*Play this as a duet with the previous exercise.*

27 **CHORALE #1 IN F MAJOR**—*Full band arrangement. Listen carefully and adjust your volume so that all the players in the ensemble may be heard. This is called balance.* **DVD**

Andante

28 **CHORALE #2 IN F MAJOR**—*Full band arrangement. Intonation is playing in tune with others. Listen carefully to achieve the best possible intonation in this chorale.* **DVD**

Moderato

29 **B♭ MAJOR SCALE AND ARPEGGIO**—*Practice at a steady tempo at various speeds to increase technical proficiency.*

30 **B♭ MAJOR SCALE INTERVAL STUDY**—*Practice at a steady tempo at various speeds to increase technical proficiency.*

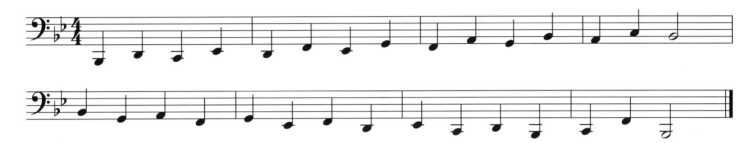

31 **CHORD BUILDER WARM-UP IN B♭ MAJOR**—*Full band arrangement. Listen carefully to how your instrument blends with the sound of the ensemble.*

32 **TONAL WARM-UP IN B♭ MAJOR**—*Listen carefully in order to play in tune and with a good tone.*

33 **TECHNICAL WARM-UP IN B♭ MAJOR**—*Play this as a duet with the previous exercise.*

34 **CHORALE #1 IN B♭ MAJOR**—*Full band arrangement. Listen carefully and adjust your volume so that all the players in the ensemble may be heard. This is called balance.*

Andante

35 **CHORALE #2 IN B♭ MAJOR**—*Full band arrangement. Intonation is playing in tune with others. Listen carefully to achieve the best possible intonation in this chorale.* (DVD)

Moderato

36 **E♭ MAJOR SCALE AND ARPEGGIO**—*Practice at a steady tempo at various speeds to increase technical proficiency.*

37 **E♭ MAJOR SCALE INTERVAL STUDY**—*Practice at a steady tempo at various speeds to increase technical proficiency.*

38 **CHORD BUILDER WARM-UP IN E♭ MAJOR**—*Full band arrangement. Listen carefully to how your instrument blends with the sound of the ensemble.*

39 **TONAL WARM-UP IN E♭ MAJOR**—*Listen carefully in order to play in tune and with a good tone.*

40 **TECHNICAL WARM-UP IN E♭ MAJOR**—*Play this as a duet with the previous exercise.*

41 **CHORALE #1 IN E♭ MAJOR**—*Full band arrangement. Listen carefully and adjust your volume so that all the players in the ensemble may be heard. This is called balance.*

42 **CHORALE #2 IN E♭ MAJOR**—*Full band arrangement. Intonation is playing in tune with others. Listen carefully to achieve the best possible intonation in this chorale.*

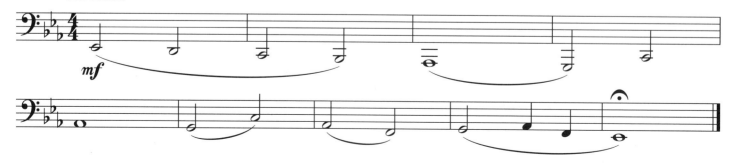

43 **A♭ MAJOR SCALE AND ARPEGGIO**—*Practice at a steady tempo at various speeds to increase technical proficiency.*

44 **A♭ MAJOR SCALE INTERVAL STUDY**—*Practice at a steady tempo at various speeds to increase technical proficiency.*

45 **CHORD BUILDER WARM-UP IN A♭ MAJOR**—*Full band arrangement. Listen carefully to how the tone of your instrument blends with the sound of the ensemble.*

46 **TONAL WARM-UP IN A♭ MAJOR**—*Listen carefully in order to play in tune and with a good tone.*

47 **TECHNICAL WARM-UP IN A♭ MAJOR**—*Play this as a duet with the previous exercise.*

48 **CHORALE #1 IN A♭ MAJOR**—*Full band arrangement. Listen carefully and adjust your volume so that all the players in the ensemble may be heard. This is called balance.*

49 **CHORALE #2 IN A♭ MAJOR**—*Full band arrangement. Intonation is playing in tune with others. Listen carefully to achieve the best possible intonation in this chorale.*

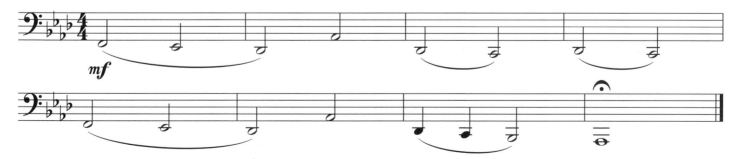

Maelzel's metronome, abbreviated M.M., uses a number to indicate the number of beats per minute on the metronome. It is often shown with a note value in place of M.M. (♩ = 108).

50 **CAVALIER REGIMENT**—*Full band arrangement. Concert march.*

Level 2: Sound Fundamentals

CUT TIME is a meter in which there are two beats per measure and the half note receives one beat. Cut time is also called **ALLA BREVE**.

$\mathbb{C} = \begin{matrix} \mathbf{2} \\ \mathbf{2} \end{matrix}$ = Two beats (counts) per measure.
= A half note receives one beat (count).

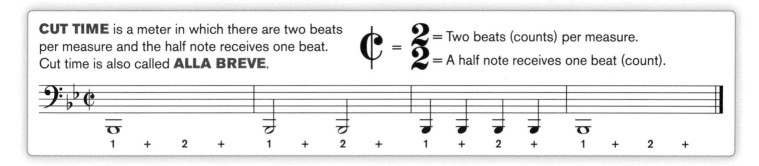

51 MAKING THE CUT—*Clap and count before you play.*

Andante

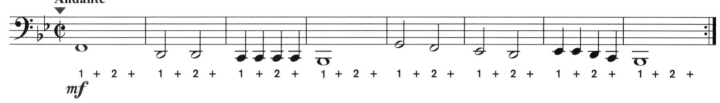

52 SOME FOLKS DO—*This version is in $\frac{2}{4}$ time.*

Stephen Foster (1826–1864)

Moderato

53 SOME FOLKS DON'T—*This version is in cut time. How is it different from the $\frac{2}{4}$ version? How is it similar?*

Stephen Foster (1826–1864)

Moderato

54 DOO-DLE IN TWO-DLE—*Play and conduct* Yankee Doodle *in common time, then change the meter to cut time by drawing a vertical line through the* $\mathbb{C}$ *(* $\mathbb{C}$ *). Now play and conduct in "two" (cut time). Both versions should sound exactly the same, but the speed of your conducting gestures will be "cut" in half!*

American Folk Song

Allegro

55 MERRILY, THIS IS HOW WE ROLL—*Play and conduct in common time, then change the meter to cut time by drawing a vertical line through the* $\mathbb{C}$ *(* $\mathbb{C}$ *). Now play and conduct in "two" (cut time). Both versions should sound exactly the same, but the speed of your conducting gestures will be "cut" in half!*

American Folk Song

Andante

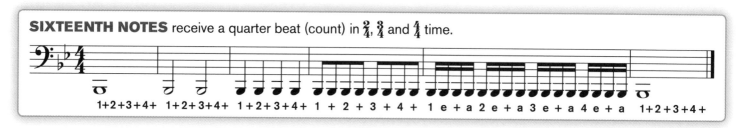

SIXTEENTH NOTES receive a quarter beat (count) in $\frac{2}{4}$, $\frac{3}{4}$ and $\frac{4}{4}$ time.

1+2+3+4+ 1+2+3+4+ 1+2+3+4+ 1 + 2 + 3 + 4 + 1 e + a 2 e + a 3 e + a 4 e + a 1+2+3+4+

56 **SWEET SIXTEENTHS!**—*Clap and count this exercise. Write in the counts under each note.*

1 + 2 + 3 e + a 4 +

57 **OATS, PEAS, BEANS**—*Use a steady stream of air to play the sixteenth notes.*

Moderato

British and American Folk Song

1 e + a 2 + 3 e + a 4+

mf

American composer and conductor **John Philip Sousa** (1854–1932) wrote many operettas, suites and songs, but he is best known as "The March King." Some of his acclaimed marches are *Semper Fidelis*, *The Washington Post*, *The Thunderer*, *El Capitan*, and his most famous composition, *Stars and Stripes Forever*.

58 **THE THUNDERER (Duet)**—*Try out your sixteenth notes with this famous march! Switch parts on the repeat.*

Alla marcia

John Philip Sousa (1854–1932)

A

B

1 + 2 e + a

f

f

1 + 2 +

A

B

59 **LISTEN TO THE MOCKINGBIRD**—*More practice with sixteenth notes.*

Moderato

Richard Milburn

mf

1 + 2 e + a

mp

mf

f

13

60 SIXTEENTH NOTES AND EIGHTH NOTES—*The combination of these notes can create the following rhythms. Clap and count.*

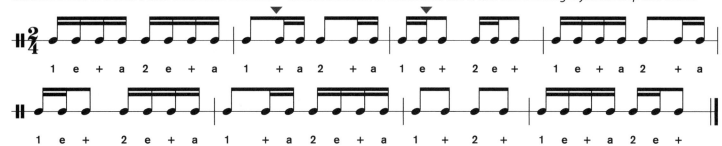

61 SIXTEENTHS GOIN' UP!—*Practice your eighth- and sixteenth-note rhythms. Play slowly, then increase the tempo as you become more comfortable tonguing the notes.*

62 EIGHTHS FALLIN' DOWN!—*Practice your sixteenth- and eighth-note rhythms. Play slowly, then increase the tempo as you become more comfortable tonguing the notes.*

63 BIG ROCK CANDY MOUNTAIN—*Practice your new eighth- and sixteenth-note combinations with this familiar song.*

American Folk Song

64 A SAILOR'S CHANTEY—*Practice eighth- and sixteenth-note combinations in 4/4 time with articulations with this familiar song.*

Traditional

65 MUSIC MARMALADE—*More practice with eighth- and sixteenth-note combinations in 3/4 time with articulations.*

66 AMERICAN PATROL—*More practice with eighth- and sixteenth-note combinations with articulations and dynamics.*

Frank W. Meacham (1850–1896)

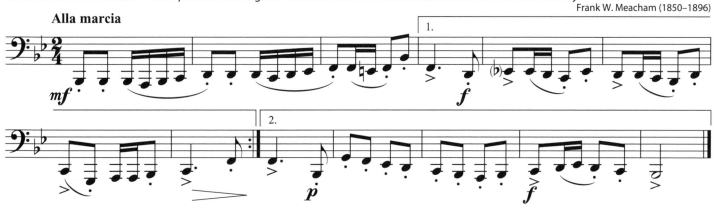

DOTTED EIGHTH NOTES receive three quarters of a beat (count) in ²/₄, ³/₄ and ⁴/₄ time.

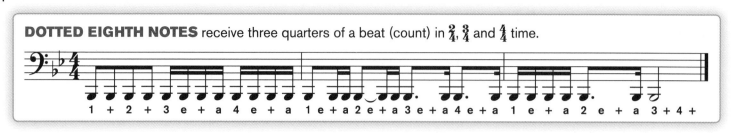

67 **ACADEMIC FESTIVAL OVERTURE**—*Practice your dotted eighth- and sixteenth-note rhythms with this famous melody.*

Johannes Brahms (1833–1897)

Maestoso

68 **BRIDAL CHORUS FROM LOHENGRIN**—*More practice using dotted eighth- and sixteenth-note rhythms.*

Richard Wagner (1813–1883)

Maestoso

69 **COUNTRY GARDENS**—*More practice using dotted eighth- and sixteenth-note rhythms.*

English Folk Song

Lightly

70 **O TANNENBAUM (Duet)**—*Here is a holiday song that uses dotted eighth- and sixteenth-note rhythms.* **DVD**

German Carol

Moderato

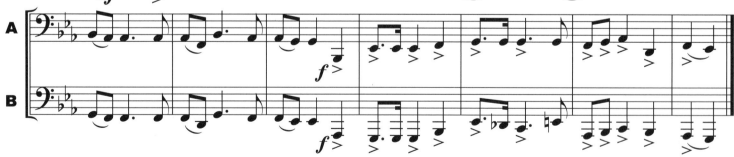

71 **ST. ANTHONY CHORALE**—*This piece uses dotted eighth- and sixteenth-note rhythms in a smooth and connected style.*

Franz Joseph Haydn (1732–1809)

Andante

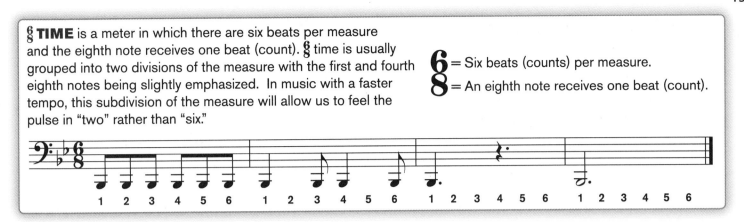

72 **THE RISING TIDE**—*Practice your $\frac{6}{8}$ meter on a concert B♭ scale. Clap the rhythms as you count the beats, then sing the piece before you play.*

73 **SIX, EIGHT, CAN'T WAIT!**—*More practice with your new $\frac{6}{8}$ rhythms. Name the key.*

74 **OVER THE RIVER AND THROUGH THE WOODS**—*Practice your new $\frac{6}{8}$ meter with this familiar tune. Play this in six until you're comfortable with the meter, then speed it up and play it in two.*

American Folk Song

75 **ROW, ROW, ROW YOUR BOAT (Round)**—*Practice your new $\frac{6}{8}$ meter with this round. Play this in six until you're comfortable with the meter, then speed it up and play it in two.*

English Folk Song

76 **I'S THE B'Y**—*Try playing this in two as you feel the bouncy style of the piece.*

Canadian Folk Song

77 **I SAW THREE SHIPS**—*This carol is in $\frac{6}{8}$ time. Play this in two.*

English Carol

EIGHTH-NOTE TRIPLETS are a group of three eighth notes played in the same space usually given to two eighth notes. In $\frac{2}{4}$, $\frac{3}{4}$ and $\frac{4}{4}$ time, an eighth-note triplet is played in one full beat with an equal division, or a third of the beat given to each note.

78 **HIPPY DIPPY TRIPLETS**—*Practice your eighth-note triplets in stepwise motion. Play this at varying speeds and dynamics.*

79 **GETTING A GRIP ON THE TRIPLET**—*Count and clap this exercise before playing it.*

80 **TRIPPING OVER THE TRIPLETS**—*Practice slowly, then increase the tempo as you become more comfortable with the technique and counting.*

81 **TRIUMPHAL MARCH FROM AIDA**—*When playing this march, be careful to make a clear distinction between the sound of the triplets and the dotted eighth- and sixteenth-note rhythms.*

Giuseppe Verdi (1813–1901)

82 **TRIPLET TARANTELLA**—*Clap this tune before you play it.*

Italian Folk Song

83 **TARANTELLA IN TWO**—*This version is in $\frac{6}{8}$, but the rhythms should sound the same as the Triplet Tarantella. Notice the difference in dynamics!*

Italian Folk Song

84   **TAKE NOTE**—*Try buzzing the pitches into the mouthpiece (without your instrument) before playing.* 🔘

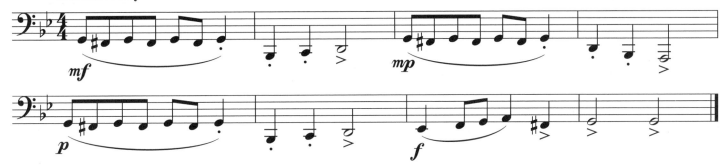

85   **SNEAKY PETE**—*Play with a full and beautiful tone at all dynamic levels. Buzz this exercise on your mouthpiece before you play.*

Mischievously

86   **PRACTICE MAKES PERFECT**

NEW NOTE   *Introducing new note D.*

87   **JOSHUA FOUGHT THE BATTLE OF JERICHO**—*Improve your technique with this spiritual. Use swing-style eighth notes in this piece!*

African-American Spiritual

Moderate swing

88   **ESTONIAN PEASANT DANCE**—*Use more air and separation on accented notes. Can you find Estonia on a map?*

Moderato

89   **Q & A**—*This tune has phrases that sound like a series of questions and answers.*

Allegro moderato

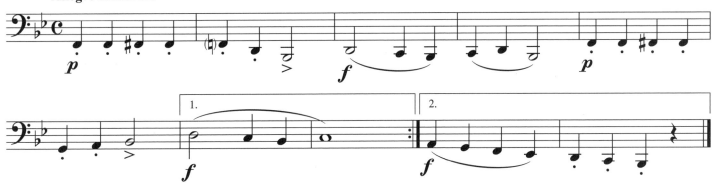

90 **SNICKERDOODLE WALTZ**—*Play this in four-measure phrases with a beautiful sound.* 🔘DVD

91 **CHOCOLATE CHIP CHA-CHA**—*Name the key.*

92 **MACEDONIAN MOUNTAIN DANCE**—*Play this in the style of a dance. Can you find Macedonia on a map?*

93 **DECK THE HALLS**—*Here's a holiday tune to help you practice your new skills. How many measures are in each phrase?*

Welsh Carol

> **Gustav Holst** (1874–1934) was an English composer known for his beautiful melodies and use of folk tunes. He is best known for his suite *The Planets*, as well as other works for orchestra, chorus, and his concert band *Suite in Eb* and *Suite in F*.

94 **IN THE BLEAK MIDWINTER**—*This tune was written by Gustav Holst. Find other examples of Holst's music to share with the class. Play this in four-measure phrases.*

Gustav Holst (1874–1934)

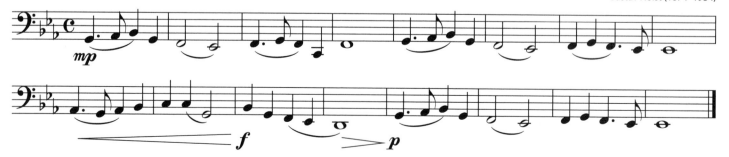

95 **CHROMATIC CRONIES**—*Practice your chromatic skills both ascending and descending.*

96 **YO-YO**—*Maintain a clear and steady tone both ascending and descending.*

97 **YO-YO PRO**—*More practice of chromatic skills both ascending and descending. Can you give the enharmonic name for each of the sharped and flatted notes in this exercise?*

98

NEW NOTES

C#/Db, Eb

YO! YOU'RE A PRO!—*More practice of your chromatic skills both ascending and descending. Can you give the enharmonic name for each of the sharped and flatted notes in this exercise?*

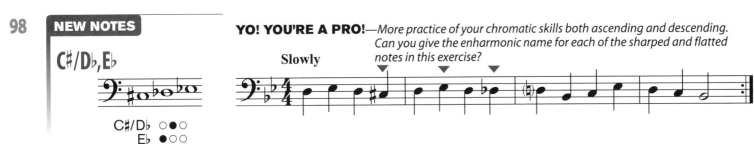

99 **PRO-LIFIC! YOU'RE TERRIFIC!**—*More practice of your chromatic skills both ascending and descending. Can you give the enharmonic name for each of the sharped and flatted notes in this exercise?*

100 **MINOR MINUET**—*This is in the key of G minor. What major key shares this key signature?*

The new key signature of **C MAJOR** tells you that all notes are natural.

101 **CONCERT C MAJOR SCALE**—*Notice the key signature and how it affects the notes you play in this key.*

102 **STRAY DOG STRUT**—*This tune gives you more practice in the key of C major.*

Proudly

103 **BEYOND THE GALAXY (Duet)**—*This tune includes accidentals in the key of C major. Switch parts on the repeat.*

Floating

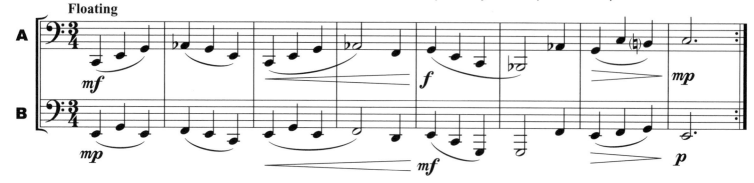

104 **LIME JUICE TUB**—*Experiment with different articulations to express this melody in differing styles. Conduct the ensemble and demonstrate the style with your conducting.* **DVD**

Australian Folk Tune

Moderato

105 **SHOO FLY!**—*Play the accents with more air and separation to help emphasize the syncopated rhythms.*

Traditional

Allegro

106 **HUNGARIAN DANCE NO. 5**—*This is one of Brahms's most famous pieces. Find other recordings of Brahms's music to share with the class. Describe some of the expressive characteristics of this piece. Vivo means to play this lively!*

Johannes Brahms (1833–1897)

Vivo!

107

NEW NOTE

ECHO CAROL—*Play the dynamics carefully to enhance the "echo."*

German Carol

Moderato

108 **NEW NOTE**   **RIDING HIGH**—*Play each note with control and a beautiful sound.*

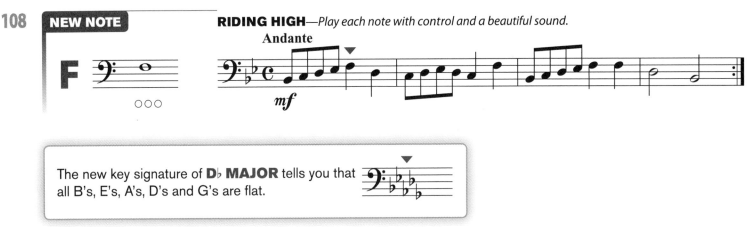

F

The new key signature of **D♭ MAJOR** tells you that all B's, E's, A's, D's and G's are flat.

109 **CONCERT D♭ MAJOR SCALE**—*Notice the key signature and how it affects the notes you play in this key.*

110 **CONCERT D♭ ETUDE**—*More practice in your new key.*

111 **MAMBO COMBO**—*This tune gives you more practice in the key of D♭ major. A mambo is a Cuban dance.*

112 **LULLABY**—*Here is another famous melody by Brahms. A lullaby is sung to help a baby go to sleep. Play this in a soothing manner.*

Johannes Brahms (1833–1897)

113 **SAILING SONG**—*Sea chanteys were sung by sailors to help them lift their spirits, as well as keep up the pace of work on the high seas. Find examples of other sea chanteys to share with the class.*

Sea Chantey

DVD *3rd valve slide should be pushed out when you play this note.*

114 NEW NOTES

FREAKY FLATS—*Here is a real brain teaser! See if you can make your way through this forest of flats!* DVD

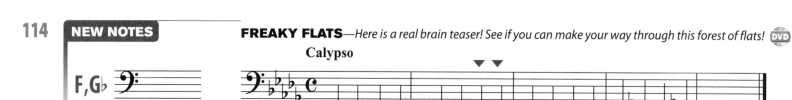

F, G♭

F ●○● G♭ ○●●

German composer **Richard Wagner** (1813–1883) is one of the most significant and influential composers of the 19th century, best known for his operas *Lohengrin*, *Tannhäuser*, and *Tristan und Isolde*, and the four-opera cycle *Der Ring des Nibelungen*.

115 **OVERTURE TO RIENZI**—*This theme is from one of Wagner's operas and provides more practice in the key of C major.*

Richard Wagner (1813–1883)

116 **ALL THROUGH THE NIGHT**—*This lovely Welsh melody provides additional practice in the key of D♭ major while having you concentrate on style and phrasing, as well as on the notes and key signature.*

Welsh Folk Song

117 **OVERTURE TO THE BARBER OF SEVILLE**—*Vivace means fast. This lively tune provides practice on scale patterns in a minor key. Careful attention to the articulation will bring out the style of the piece.*

Gioachino Rossini (1792–1868)

118 **OVERTURE TO DIE MEISTERSINGER**—*This theme is from another of Wagner's most famous operas. Find other music of Wagner to share with the class.*

Richard Wagner (1813–1883)

119 **AFRICAN ADVENTURE**—*Full band arrangement.*

120 **THE WATER IS WIDE**—*Full band arrangement.*

Slowly with expression (♩ = 84)

English Folk Song

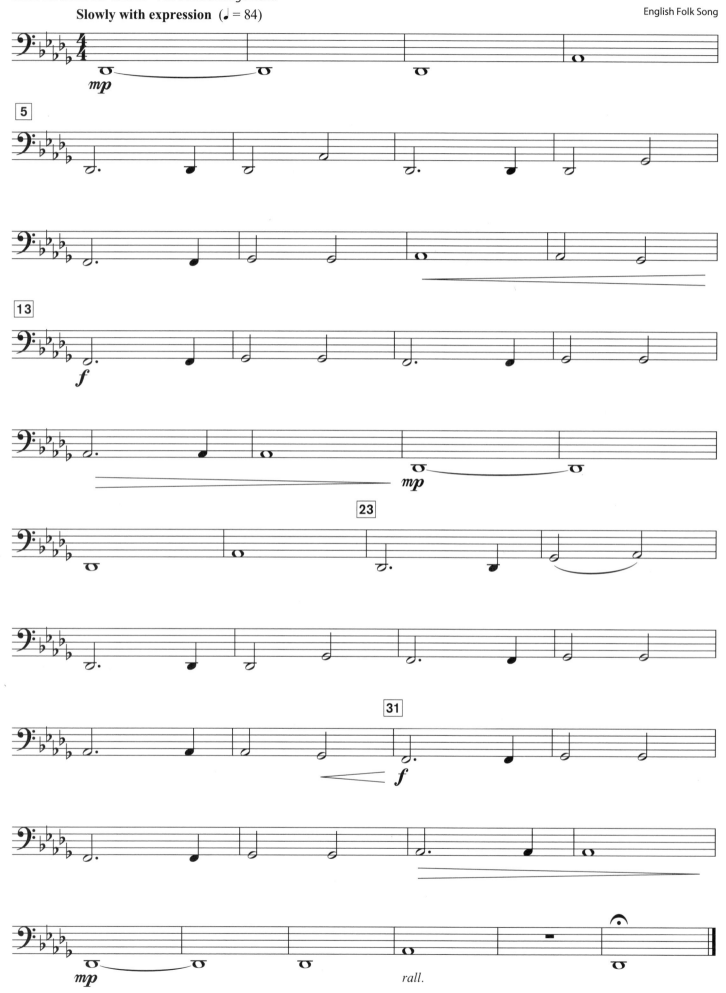

▶ Complete the **SOUND CHECK** near the end of your book.

Level 3: Sound Development

121 RISE AND FALL—*Practice your chromatic skills. What are the enharmonic names of the notes with accidentals?*

122 CHILL OUT CHA-CHA-CHA—*This Cuban dance follows the rhythm pattern of the güiro on beats 3 and 4, which sounds like "cha-cha-cha."
Name the enharmonics for the notes with accidentals before you play.*

123 THE GOOD KING'S DUET—*Switch parts on the repeat of this holiday duet.*

Christmas Carol

SIGHT-READING is the ability to play a piece of music from beginning to end without having seen or practiced it. This requires calling upon all of your musical skills at once while concentrating on reading and playing with expression. Prepare to sight read by examining the following before you play:

- key signature
- meter
- style and tempo
- "roadmap" of the piece
- dynamics

- notes
- rhythms
- accidentals
- articulation
- composer and title

---

124 CORONATION MARCH—*Sight-reading exercise.*

125 CARIBBEAN CRUISE—*Sight-reading exercise.*

26

German composer **Johann Pachelbel** (1653–1706), best known for his works for organ, was an important composer of the Baroque period. Undoubtedly, his most famous work is his *Canon in D.*

A **CANON** is a compositional technique in which several voices or instruments play the same music but begin at different times, creating interesting harmonies. A round is a type of canon.

126 **PACHELBEL'S CANON**—*Play this like a round. Repeat as desired. End the piece by holding the first note of any of the four-measure phrases.*

Andante

Johann Pachelbel (1653–1706)

ALLEGRETTO is a moderately fast tempo, not quite as fast as Allegro.

127 **REUBEN AND RACHEL (Round)**—*Try out your new tempo with this familiar tune.*

▶Allegretto

Traditional

There are three kinds of **MINOR KEYS**—Natural Minor, Harmonic Minor and Melodic Minor.

Major Scale

Natural Minor Scale (lower 3rd, 6th and 7th notes)

Harmonic Minor Scale (lower 3rd and 6th, but 7th remains raised)

The Melodic Minor Scale changes depending on direction. When ascending only the 3rd is lowered, but descending lowers the 3rd, 6th and 7th.

128 **NATURALLY MINOR REUBEN AND RACHEL (Round)**—*Compare the sound of this tune to the previous line. How is it the same? How is it different? In the previous line of music, Reuben and Rachel was in a major key. This is in a minor key. What major key shares this key signature?*

Allegretto

Traditional

129 **CAMPTOWN RACES**—*More practice in Allegretto tempo.*

Allegretto

Stephen Foster (1826–1864)

130 **TRANSPOSING** is changing a piece of music by starting it on a different pitch (note). Have your teacher help you transpose the first three measures below, starting on the first notes in measures four and seven, then play.

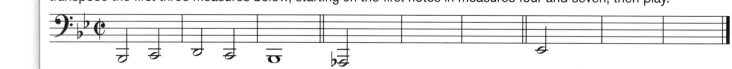

More Dynamics! **FORTISSIMO** (*ff*) is very loud. **PIANISSIMO** (*pp*) is very soft.

EIGHTH NOTES BEAMED OVER A REST often occur in 6/8 time and in eighth-note triplets. Clap each line below before playing to help you feel comfortable with this concept and notation.

131 **IN DULCE JUBILO**—*Practice your new dynamics.* (DVD)

Christmas Carol

132 **POP! GOES THE WEASEL**—*More practice using dynamics.*

English Folk Song

133 **WHEN JOHNNY COMES MARCHING HOME**—*More dynamic practice.*

American Civil War Song

134 **YE BANKS AND BRAES**—Fortissimo *playing requires control over your tone quality. While this tune uses a large dynamic range, work to play with beauty and sensitivity throughout.* (DVD)

Robert Burns (1759–1796)

135 **RAZZLE-DAZZLE RHYTHM RIDDLES**—*Here are some more rhythms in 6/8 time for you to "solve." Clap and count before you play.*

A TEMPO means "in time." The term is used to indicate the return to the tempo prior to a change in the pace of the music such as a *rallentando*.

136 **FOR HE'S A JOLLY GOOD FELLOW**—*Circle the A tempo before you play.*

137 **GOOD MORNING TO ALL**—*More practice with A tempo.*

A **CHORD** is a group of harmonically-related notes played together. The most common type of chord is a triad. Triads can be created by playing the 1st, 3rd and 5th notes of a scale, which creates a major chord. The 2nd, 4th and 6th notes create a minor chord. With two friends, try creating triads on other scale notes to experiment with creating other chords.

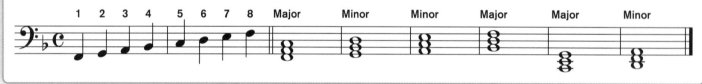

138 **AMAZING GRACE**—*Before playing, assign an equal number of players to each note in the final chord.*

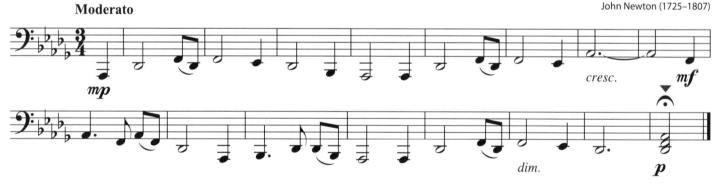

139 **MORE FUN WITH CHORDS**—*On each of the whole notes, choose one of the notes in the chord to play. Listen for the harmony.*

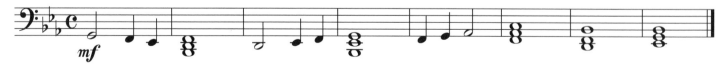

140 **MORE FUN WITH SIXTEENTH NOTES AND RESTS**—*Here is a rhythm challenge! Clap before you play.*

▶ Complete the **SOUND CHECK** near the end of your book.

141 **AU CLAIR DE LA LUNE**—*Not all sixteenth notes are played at a fast tempo. Practice your sixteenth notes with this familiar tune at a slow tempo.*

French Folk Song

German composer **Carl Maria von Weber** (1786–1826) was a significant and influential composer of the Romantic period, best known for his operas *Der Freischütz*, *Oberon* and *Euryanthe*.

142 **HUNTER'S CHORUS**—*Here is additional sixteenth-note practice on this famous melody.*

Carl Maria von Weber (1786–1826)

143 **SHEPHERD'S HEY (Duet)**—*More sixteenth-note fun with this duet. Switch parts on the repeat.*

English Folk Song

LEGATO STYLE means to play notes full-value in a smooth, connected manner without clipping phrase endings.

144 **AWAY IN A MANGER**—*This traditional carol is best played in* legato *style.*

Traditional Carol

145 **ERIE CANAL**—Pesante *means heavy. Discuss with your teacher ways you can make this sound "heavy."*

Thomas Allen (1876–1919)

▶ Pesante

146 **STODOLA PUMPA**—*A polka is a Polish dance, popular throughout eastern Europe. Practice light and separated sixteenth notes with this polka.*

Czech Folk Song

Lightly

147 **REVEILLE**—*This familiar bugle call will help you practice sixteenth-note rhythms. If practiced at home very early in the day, it will also help your family get out of bed in the morning!*

Military Bugle Call

Vivo!

A **COUNTERMELODY** is a musical line that has its own tune, but can be played along with another melody to create interesting harmonies.

American organist and composer **Samuel Augustus Ward** (1847–1903) is best known for writing the music to "America, the Beautiful," with lyrics by the poet Katharine Lee Bates.

148 **AMERICA, THE BEAUTIFUL (Duet)**—*This duet includes a melody and a countermelody. Before playing, can you find where the melody is used as part of the countermelody?*

Samuel A. Ward (1847–1903)

Andante

149 **ALOUETTE**—*This familiar song is written with dotted eighth- and sixteenth-note rhythms.*

French-Canadian Folk Song

150 **HAIL TO THE CHIEF**—*Dotted eighth- and sixteenth-note rhythms can add a majestic quality to music. This tune is used to announce the arrival of the President of the United States.*

James Sanderson (1769–1841)

151 **ADVANCE, AUSTRALIA FAIR**—*This is the Australian National Anthem.*

Peter Dodds McCormick (1834–1916)

152 **KUM BA YAH**—*This familiar tune uses* legato *style dotted eighth- and sixteenth-note rhythms.*

African-American Spiritual

153 **TAPS**—*This bugle call uses* legato *style dotted eighth- and sixteenth-note rhythms.*

Daniel Butterfield (1831–1901)

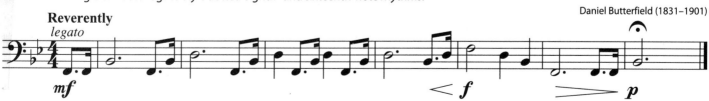

Russian composer **Pyotr Ilyich Tchaikovsky** (1840–1893), considered one of the most significant composers of the Romantic period, is best known for his symphonies, the *1812 Overture* and the ballets *Swan Lake*, *The Nutcracker* and *The Sleeping Beauty*.

A **TWO-MEASURE REPEAT** ($\overset{2}{\mathcal{X}\mathpunct{:}}$) is a symbol that tells you to repeat the previous two measures.

154 **MARCH FROM THE NUTCRACKER**—*This well-known melody uses eighth-note triplets and a two-measure repeat.*

Pyotr Ilyich Tchaikovsky (1840–1893)

f–*p* means to play forte the first time and piano on the repeat. Notice that the *f*–*p* looks similar to *fp*, so don't get them confused! Other dynamics can be used as well, such as *p*–*f* or *mp*–*mf*.

155 **PROCESSION OF THE ELDERS**—*Practice your two-measure repeats and the change of dynamics on the second time through the piece.*

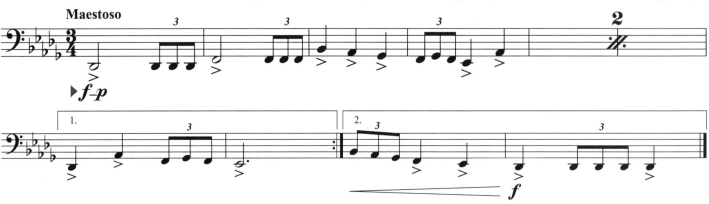

156 **REPEATIN' THE BLUES**—*Practice one-measure and two-measure repeats. Look at your dynamics!*

157 **THE BATTLE HYMN OF THE REPUBLIC**—*Practice the change of dynamics on the repeat. Can you play the rest of the song by "ear"?*

William Steffe (1830–1890)

▶ Complete the **SOUND CHECK** near the end of your book.

D.C. AL CODA means to repeat from the beginning (*da capo* or "head") and then play the *coda* (the "tail") where indicated.

158 THE IRISH JAUNTING CAR—*Trace the "roadmap" of the piece before you play.*

Irish Folk Song

GRACE NOTES are a type of musical ornamentation. They are placed prior to and are slurred to the note they enhance, and appear smaller in size. Grace notes usually are single notes, either with or without a slash through the stem and flag, but can also include two or more notes. Rhythmically they are placed immediately prior to the beat, but in music of the Baroque and Early Classical periods they are sometimes played on the beat.

159 GOODNESS, GRACE NOTES!—*Try out your grace notes. Make sure they feel relaxed and not forced.* 🅓🅥🅓

160 TRAVELIN' TO ARKANSAS—*A hoedown is an American folk dance. Play the grace notes lightly and just before the beat of the note they precede.*

161 GRACEFUL GRACE NOTES—*Here are more grace notes to practice. Make sure they have a natural and relaxed feel to them and never sound rushed.*

162 **HORNPIPE FROM WATER MUSIC**—*This popular tune uses syncopation and changing dynamics.*

George Frideric Handel (1685–1759)

ADAGIO is a tempo marking that indicates the music is to be played very slowly.

SFORZANDO or *sfz* indicates a strong, sudden accent.

163 **SPOOKY SFORZANDOS**—*Practice your* sforzando *accents on this slow and scary tune.*

164 **WHERE'ER YOU WALK**—*Practice playing* Adagio *with this stately aria.*

George Frideric Handel (1685–1759)

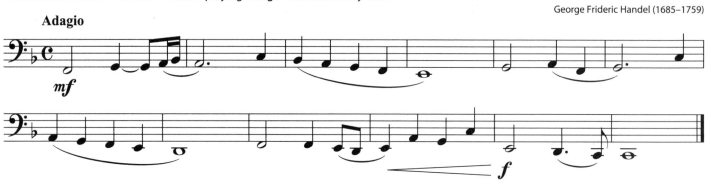

The key signature can change during a piece of music. When this happens a double bar will precede the key change. Any flats or sharps that are "cancelled" as a result of the new key signature may be indicated with a natural sign.

165 **SAILING THROUGH THE KEYS**—*Name the two key signatures included in this piece.*

D.S. AL CODA means to repeat from the sign (*dal segno*) 𝄋 and then go to the *Coda* 𝄌 where indicated.

ANDANTINO is a moderate tempo, slightly faster than *Andante*.

166 STAR OF THE COUNTY DOWN—*Trace the "roadmap" of the piece before you play.*

Irish Folk Tune

167 ROCK THE CRADLE JOE—*This tune offers more practice opportunities with D.S. al Coda.*

American Fiddle Tune

168 OLIVER JACK (Duet)—*This includes a D.S. al Coda.*

Scottish Folk Song

36

The word **MOLTO** means "very." **MOLTO RALLENTANDO** (*molto rall.*) and **MOLTO RITARDANDO** (*molto rit.*) mean to progressively slow the tempo dramatically. The word **POCO** means "little." **POCO RALLENTANDO** (*poco rall.*) and **POCO RITARDANDO** (*poco rit.*) mean to progressively slow the tempo just a little.

169 ANNIE LAURIE—*Notice the tempo markings before you play.*

Scottish Folk Song

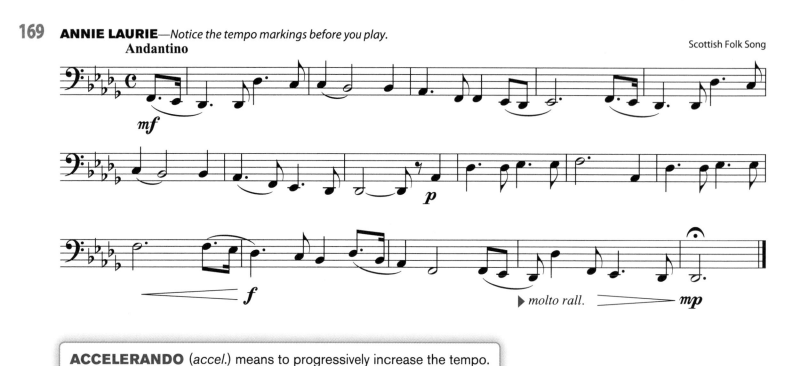

ACCELERANDO (*accel.*) means to progressively increase the tempo.

170 ROLLING DOWN THE HILL—*Practice playing an* accelerando. *Use the tempo change to create a musical representation of the title.*

171 COASTING TO A STOP—*Practice playing a* poco rallentando. *Use the tempo change to create a musical representation of the title.*

A **MARCATO ACCENT** (∧) is a strong, short accent.

172 MEXICAN HAT ACCENTS—*Try out your* marcato *accents with this familiar tune.* 🅳🆅🅳

Mexican Folk Dance

▶ Complete the **SOUND CHECK** near the end of your book.

173 VARIATIONS ON AN ENGLISH FOLK SONG—*Solo* DVD

Piano Accompaniment

Level 4: Sound Musicianship

The following two pages provide a complete and total assessment of everything learned in Book 2. If you can play through these six exercises and understand the terms in the glossary, you have accomplished and mastered all of the goals, concepts, key signatures and rhythms presented in this book. You can consider this to be your All-in-One Assessment!

174 **COMPREHENSIVE ASSESSMENT IN D MAJOR (CONCERT C)**—*This exercise includes* $\frac{4}{4}$ *time, sixteenth notes, A Tempo,* f–p *and molto rall.*

175 **COMPREHENSIVE ASSESSMENT IN CONCERT F MAJOR**—*This exercise includes* $\frac{3}{4}$ *time, eighth- and two-sixteenth note rhythms, syncopation, D.C. al Coda and accelerando.*

176 **COMPREHENSIVE ASSESSMENT IN CONCERT B♭ MAJOR**—*This exercise includes* $\frac{2}{4}$ *time, dotted eighth- and sixteenth-notes, grace notes and a chord.*

177 **COMPREHENSIVE ASSESSMENT IN CONCERT E♭ MAJOR**—*This exercise includes common time, triplets, triplets with rests, and an Adagio tempo.*

178 **COMPREHENSIVE ASSESSMENT IN CONCERT A♭ MAJOR**—*This exercise includes cut time and legato-style playing. It can also be played as a canon. Note the entrance points for each part. The piece can end by holding the 1st note of any eight-measure phrase.*

179 **COMPREHENSIVE ASSESSMENT IN CONCERT D♭ MAJOR**—*This exercise reinforces ⁶⁄₈ time (in six and in two), **pp**, **ff**, two-measure repeats, marcato accents, Andantino and D.S. al Coda.*

180 **CONCERT C MAJOR SCALE AND ARPEGGIO**—*Listen carefully in order to play in tune and with a good tone.*

181 **CONCERT A MINOR SCALE AND ARPEGGIO**—*Listen carefully in order to play in tune and with a good tone.*

182 **TECHNICAL SCALE ETUDE IN CONCERT C MAJOR**—*Play slowly until you are comfortable with the technique, then play at a faster tempo.*

183 **CHORALE IN CONCERT C MAJOR**—*Full band arrangement. Listen to all of the other instruments and work to achieve blend and balance.*

Andante ($\quad$ = 72)

184 **CONCERT F MAJOR SCALE AND ARPEGGIO**—*Listen carefully in order to play in tune and with a good tone.*

185 **CONCERT D MINOR SCALE AND ARPEGGIO**—*Listen carefully in order to play in tune and with a good tone.*

186 **TECHNICAL SCALE ETUDE IN CONCERT F MAJOR**—*Play slowly until you are comfortable with the technique, then play at a faster tempo.*

187 **CHORALE IN CONCERT F MAJOR**—*Full band arrangement. Listen to all of the other instruments and work to achieve blend and balance.*

Andante ($\quad$ = 72)

188 **CONCERT B♭ MAJOR SCALE AND ARPEGGIO**—*Listen carefully in order to play in tune and with a good tone.*

189 **CONCERT G MINOR SCALE AND ARPEGGIO**—*Listen carefully in order to play in tune and with a good tone.*

190 **TECHNICAL SCALE ETUDE IN CONCERT B♭ MAJOR**—*Play slowly until you are comfortable with the technique, then play at a faster tempo.*

191 **CHORALE IN CONCERT B♭ MAJOR**—*Full band arrangement. Listen to all of the other instruments and work to achieve blend and balance.*

Andante (♩ = 72)

192 **CONCERT E♭ MAJOR SCALE AND ARPEGGIO**—*Listen carefully in order to play in tune and with a good tone.*

193 **CONCERT C MINOR SCALE AND ARPEGGIO**—*Listen carefully in order to play in tune and with a good tone.*

194 **TECHNICAL SCALE ETUDE IN CONCERT E♭ MAJOR**—*Play slowly until you are comfortable with the technique, then play at a faster tempo.*

195 **CHORALE IN CONCERT E♭ MAJOR**—*Full band arrangement. Listen to all of the other instruments and work to achieve blend and balance.*

Andante (♩ = 72)

196 **CONCERT A♭ MAJOR SCALE AND ARPEGGIO**—*Listen carefully in order to play in tune and with a good tone.*

197 **CONCERT F MINOR SCALE AND ARPEGGIO**—*Listen carefully in order to play in tune and with a good tone.*

198 **TECHNICAL SCALE ETUDE IN CONCERT A♭ MAJOR**—*Play slowly until you are comfortable with the technique, then play at a faster tempo.*

199 **CHORALE IN CONCERT A♭ MAJOR**—*Full band arrangement. Listen to all of the other instruments and work to achieve blend and balance.*

Andante (♩ = 72)

200 **CONCERT D♭ MAJOR SCALE AND ARPEGGIO**—*Listen carefully in order to play in tune and with a good tone.*

201 **CONCERT B♭ MINOR SCALE AND ARPEGGIO**—*Listen carefully in order to play in tune and with a good tone.*

202 **TECHNICAL SCALE ETUDE IN CONCERT D♭ MAJOR**—*Play slowly until you are comfortable with the technique, then play at a faster tempo.*

203 **CHORALE IN CONCERT D♭ MAJOR**—*Full band arrangement. Listen to all of the other instruments and work to achieve blend and balance.*

Andante (♩ = 72)

204 RHYTHMS IN $\frac{4}{4}$ TIME

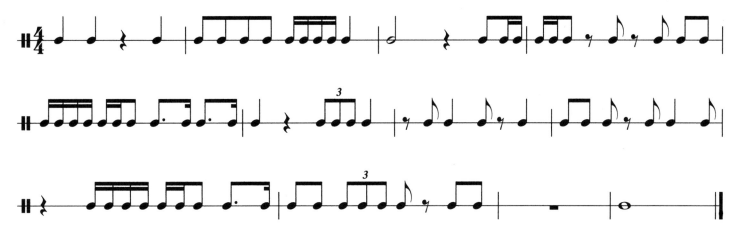

205 RHYTHMS IN $\frac{3}{4}$ TIME

206 RHYTHMS IN $\frac{2}{4}$ TIME

207 RHYTHMS IN COMMON TIME

208 RHYTHMS IN CUT TIME

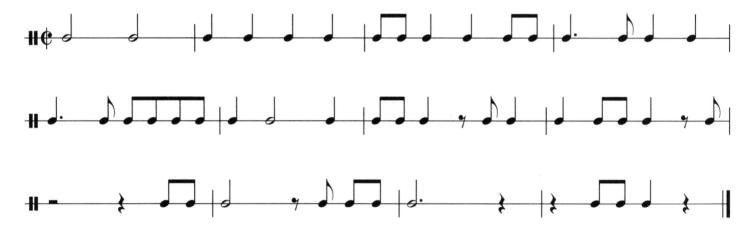

209 RHYTHMS IN $\frac{6}{8}$ TIME

Sound Check

Level 2
Check off each skill you have mastered.

___ Cut time

___ Sixteenth notes

___ Dotted eighth notes

___ $\frac{6}{8}$ time

___ Eighth-note triplet

Level 3 (Emphasis on Meter)
Check off each skill you have mastered.

___ Sight-reading

___ Canon

___ Allegretto

___ Minor scale

___ Dynamics (*ff*, *pp*)

___ Eighth notes beamed over a rest

___ A tempo

___ Chord

Level 3 (Emphasis on Rhythm)
Check off each skill you have mastered.

___ Legato style playing

___ Countermelody

___ Two-measure repeat

___ Forte-piano (*f–p*)

Level 3 (Emphasis on Key Signature)
Check off each skill you have mastered.

___ D.C. al Coda

___ Grace notes

___ Adagio

___ Sforzando

___ Key change

___ Poco rallentando

___ D.S. al Coda

___ Andantino

___ Molto rallentando

___ Accelerando

___ Marcato accent

Tuba Fingering Chart

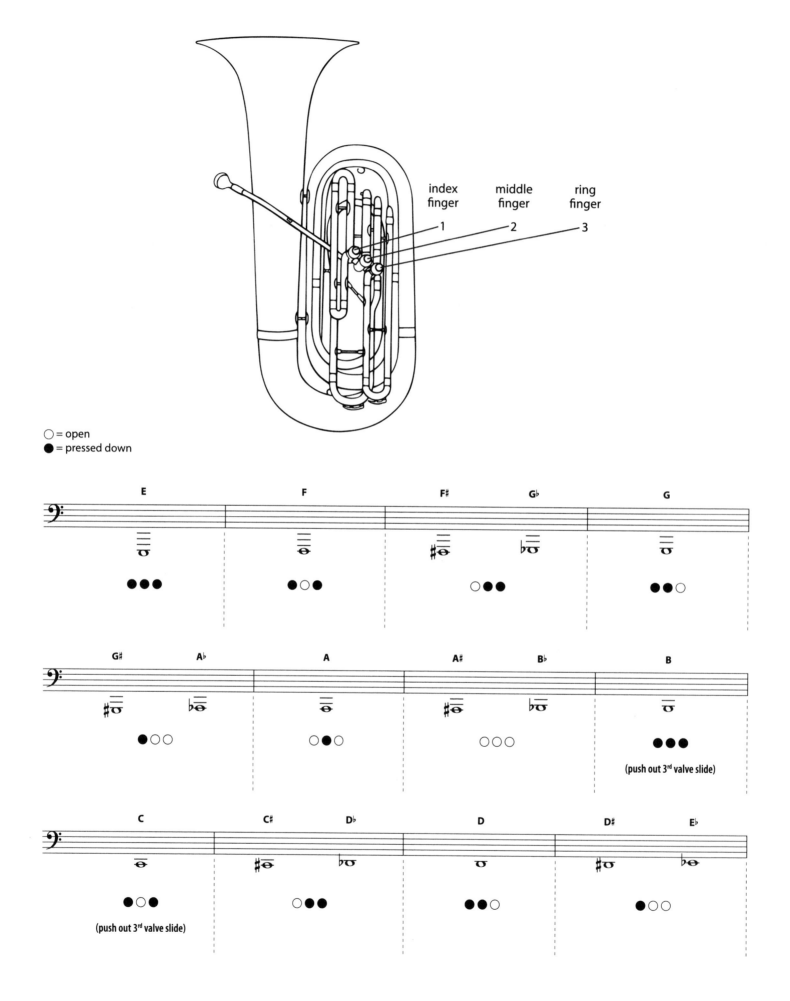

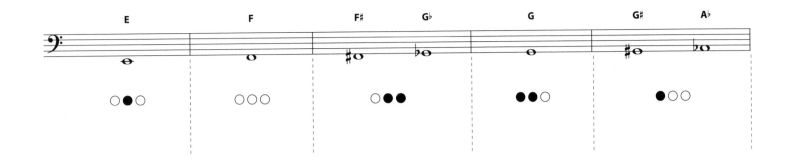

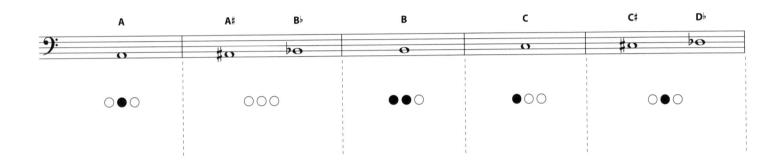

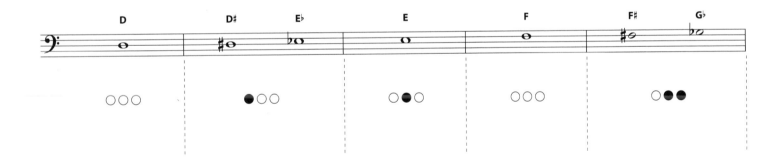

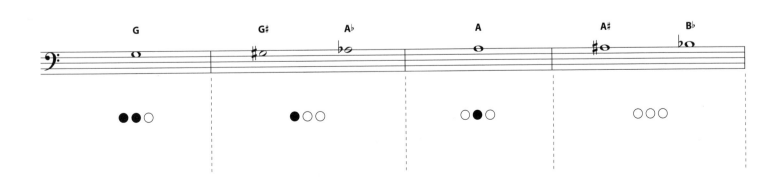

48

Glossary

a tempo – return to the original tempo

accelerando – becoming gradually faster

accompaniment – a part that provides harmony

adagio – a slow tempo, slower than *andante*

alla marcia – play in the style of a march

allegretto – to play in a lively, quick manner that is slower than *allegro*

allegro – a fast tempo

andante – a moderate walking tempo

andantino – a slow tempo, slightly faster than *andante*

arpeggio – the notes of a chord played one after another

articulation – indicates how a note should be played

balance – occurs when performers adjust their volume so all players in the ensemble may be heard

blend – occurs when performers adjust the tone of their instruments so the combined ensemble produces a beautiful sound

blues – an American art form derived from spirituals and work songs; it is the root of rock and roll, bluegrass and jazz

breath mark – tells you to take a deep breath through your mouth

calypso – a style of music from Trinidad popular in the United States during the late 1950s and early 60s

canon – where one melody begins, followed at a specific interval of time by the same melody note for note

cha-cha-cha – a Latin-American dance with an insistent rhythm

chord – three or more tones sounded simultaneously

countermelody – composing with two or more melodies played simultaneously; literally "note against note"

cut time – $\frac{2}{2}$ meter; sometimes the time signature (¢) is used

D.C. al Coda – repeat from the beginning and play to the "To Coda" (θ), then skip to the *Coda*

D.C. al Fine – repeat from the beginning and play to the *Fine*

dotted eighth notes – receive three quarters of a beat (count) in $\frac{2}{4}$, $\frac{3}{4}$ and $\frac{4}{4}$ time

D.S. al Coda – repeat from the sign (𝄋) and play to the "To Coda" (θ), then skip to the *Coda*

D.S. al Fine – repeat from the sign (𝄋) and play to the *Fine*

duet – a composition for two performers

enharmonic – refers to two notes that sound the same and use the same fingering but are written differently

etude – a "study" piece, or an exercise that helps you practice a specific technique

fermata (𝄐) – hold a note or rest longer than its normal duration

Fine – the end of a piece of music

forte-piano ($f\text{-}p$) – indicates to play forte the first time, and piano on the repeat; any dynamics may be used

fortissimo ($f\!f$) – play very loud

grace note – a small note played quickly before the beat

hoedown – a quick dance featuring fancy footwork associated with rural America

intonation – the ability to play or sing in tune

largo – a slow tempo

ledger line – short, horizontal line used to extend the staff either higher or lower

legato (–) – an articulation or style of playing that is smooth and connected

legato style playing – to play or sing groups of notes smoothly and without separate attacks

lightly – playing in a style that is not accented, loud or heavy

Maelzel's metronome (**M.M.**) – a number which indicates the number of beats per minute

maestoso – to play in a majestic manner

mambo – a West-Indian ballroom dance similar to the cha-cha-cha and rumba

marcato (∧) – an accented or stressed note

minor scale – a series of ascending and/or descending notes spanning an octave representing a minor key, always including a lowered (minor) 3rd degree of the scale

moderato – a medium tempo

molto rallentando – becoming much slower

molto ritardando – becoming much slower

pesante – heavy

pianissimo (pp) – play very softly

poco rallentando – becoming a little slower

poco ritardando – becoming a little slower

polka – a fast Bohemian dance in duple time that originated around 1830

rallentando – becoming gradually slower

ritardando – becoming gradually slower

sforzando (sf or sfz) – a sudden or strong accent

sight-reading – to play a piece for the first time

$\frac{6}{8}$ time – a meter in which there are six beats per measure and an eighth note receives one beat. It is most often played at a faster tempo in which it feels as if there are two beats per measure with the dotted quarter receiving one beat

sixteenth note – a note half the length of an eighth note

staccato (·) – an articulation or style of playing that is light and separated

swing – a style of big band jazz music popular in the 1930s and 40s

syncopation – occurs when there is emphasis on a weak beat

transpose – changing a composition from one key to another

triplet – three notes played in the time of two of the same value

two-measure repeat ($\frac{2}{\text{\textit{//}}}$) – repeat the two previous measures

vivace – lively, quick

vivo – lively and spirited

waltz – a popular dance in $\frac{3}{4}$ time